AGAINST

LOVE

POETRY

ALSO BY EAVAN BOLAND

New Territory

The War Horse

Night Feed

The Journey

Selected Poems: 1989

Outside History: Selected Poems, 1980–1990

In a Time of Violence

An Origin Like Water: Collected Poems 1967–1987

The Lost Land

Object Lessons: The Life of the Woman and the Poet in Our Time

The Making of a Poem (edited with Mark Strand)

AGAINST

LOVE

POETRY

Eavan Boland

W. W. Norton & Company

New York London

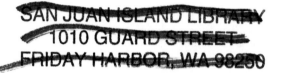
Copyright © 2001 by Eavan Boland

The text of this book is composed in Bodoni Light
with the display set in Bodoni Medium
Composition by AW Bennett Inc.
Manufacturing by Courier Companies, Inc.
Book design by JAM Design
Production manager: Leelo Märjamaa-Reintal

Library of Congress Cataloging-in-Publication Data

Boland, Eavan.
Against love poetry / by Eavan Boland.
p. cm.
ISBN 0-393-02042-8
1. Married people—Poetry. 2. Marriage—Poetry. I. Title.

PR6052.O35 A72 2001
821'.914-dc21   2001030698

W. W. Norton & Company, Inc., 500 Fifth Avenue, New York, N.Y. 10110
www.wwnorton.com

W. W. Norton & Company Ltd., Castle House, 75/76 Wells Street, London W1T 3QT

1 2 3 4 5 6 7 8 9 0

Acknowledgments are made to the editors of the following
publications, where some of these poems first appeared:

The Atlantic Monthly
The Paris Review
The Yale Review
Threepenny Review
PN Review
The Tribune
New Hibernia Review
Poetry
Antioch Review

The following poems originally appeared in *The New Yorker:*

"Quarantine"
"First Year"
"Thanked Be Fortune"
"Lines for a Thirtieth Wedding Anniversary"
"A Marriage for the Millennium"

"Limits I and II" appeared in a limited edition as "Limitations,"
published by Dim Gray Bar Press, New York.

My thanks to Jill Bialosky,
Jody Allen-Randolph,
and Kevin Casey.

FOR MY HUSBAND, KEVIN

CONTENTS

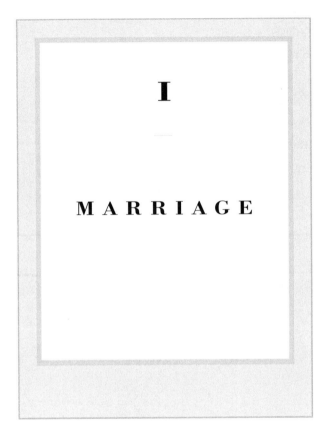

I

MARRIAGE

1. IN WHICH HESTER BATEMAN, 18TH CENTURY ENGLISH SILVERSMITH, TAKES AN IRISH COMMISSION

Hester Bateman made a marriage spoon
And then subjected it to violence.
Chased, beat it. Scarred it and marked it.
All in the spirit of our darkest century.

Far away from grapeshot and tar caps
And the hedge schools and the music of sedition
She is oblivious to she pours out
And lets cool the sweet colonial metal.

Here in miniature a man and woman
Emerge beside each other from the earth,
From the deep mine, from the seams of rock
Which made inevitable her craft of hurt.

They stand side by side on the handle.
She writes their names in the smooth
Mimicry of a lake the ladle is making, in
A flowing script with a moon drowned in it.

Art and marriage: now a made match.
The silver bends and shines and in its own
Mineral curve an age-old tension
Inches towards the light. See how

Past and future and the space between
The semblance of empire, the promise of nation,
Are vanishing in this mediation
Between oppression and love's remembrance

Until resistance is their only element. It is
What they embody, bound now and always.
History frowns on them: yet in its gaze
They join their injured hands and make their vows.

II. AGAINST LOVE POETRY

We were married in summer, thirty years ago. I have loved you deeply from that moment to this. I have loved other things as well. Among them the idea of women's freedom. Why do I put these words side by side? Because I am a woman. Because marriage is not freedom. Therefore, every word here is written against love poetry. Love poetry can do no justice to this. Here, instead, is a remembered story from a faraway history: A great king lost a war and was paraded in chains through the city of his enemy. They taunted him. They brought his wife and children to him—he showed no emotion. They brought his former courtiers—he showed no emotion. They brought his old servant—only then did he break down and weep. I did not find my womanhood in the servitudes of custom. But I saw my humanity look back at me there. It is to mark the contradictions of a daily love that I have written this. Against love poetry.

III. THE PINHOLE CAMERA

solar eclipse, August 1999

This is the day
    and in preparation
        you punch a hole
in a piece of card.
    You hold it up against
a sheet of paper—
        the simplest form
    of a pinhole camera—
        and put the sun
on your right shoulder:
        A bright disc
appears on your page.
    It loses half its diameter.
    And more than half
in another minute.
    You know
the reason for the red berries
darkening, and the road outside
    darkening, but did you know
        that the wedding
    of light and gravity
        is forever?
The sun is in eclipse:
    if this were legend

6

the king of light would turn his face away.
A single shadow
would kill the salmon-rich
rivers and birdlife
and lilac of this island.
But this is real—
how your page records
the alignment of planets:
their governance.
In other words,
the not-to-be-seen-again
mystery of
a mutual influence:
The motorways
are flowing north.
The sycamores are a perfect green.
The wild jasmine
is a speaking white.
The sun is coming back. As
it will. As it must.
You track its progress.
I stand and watch.
For you and I
such science holds no secrets:

We are married thirty years,
woman and man.
Long enough
to know about power and nature.
Long enough
to know which is which.

IV. QUARANTINE

In the worst hour of the worst season
    of the worst year of a whole people
a man set out from the workhouse with his wife.
He was walking—they were both walking—north.

She was sick with famine fever and could not keep up.
    He lifted her and put her on his back.
He walked like that west and west and north.
Until at nightfall under freezing stars they arrived.

In the morning they were both found dead.
    Of cold. Of hunger. Of the toxins of a whole history.
But her feet were held against his breastbone.
The last heat of his flesh was his last gift to her.

Let no love poem ever come to this threshold.
    There is no place here for the inexact
praise of the easy graces and sensuality of the body.
There is only time for this merciless inventory:

Their death together in the winter of 1847.
    Also what they suffered. How they lived.
And what there is between a man and woman.
And in which darkness it can best be proved.

V. EMBERS

One night in winter when a bitter frost
made the whin-paths crack underfoot
a wretched woman, eyes staring, hair in disarray,
came to the place where the Fianna had pitched camp.

Your face is made of shadow. You are reading.
There is heat from the fire still. I am reading:

She asked every one of them in turn
to take her to his bed, to shelter her with his body.
Each one looked at her—she was old beyond her years.
Each one refused her, each spurned her, except Diarmuid.

When he woke in the morning she was young and beautiful.
And she was his, forever, but on one condition.
He could not say that she had once been old and haggard.
He could not say that she had ever . . . here I look up.

You are turned away. You have no interest in this.

I made this fire from the first peat of winter.
Look at me in the last, burnished light of it.
Tell me that you feel the warmth still.
Tell me you will never speak about the ashes.

VI. THEN

Where are the lives we lived
when we were young?
Our kisses, the heat of our skin, our bitter words?
The first waking to the first child's cry?

VII. FIRST YEAR

It was our first home—
our damp, upstairs,
one-year eyrie—
above a tree-lined area
nearer the city.

My talkative, unsure,
unsettled self
was everywhere;
but you
were the clear spirit of somewhere.

At night
when we settled down
in the big bed by the window,
over the streetlight
and the first crackle of spring

eased the iron at
the base of the railings,
unpacking crocuses,
it was
the awkward corners of your snowy town

which filled
the rooms we made
and stayed there all year with
the burnt-orange lampshade,
the wasps in the attic.

Where is the soul of a marriage?

Because I am writing this
not to recall our lives,
but to imagine them,
I will say it is
in the first gifts of place:

the steep inclines
and country silences
of your boyhood,
the orange-faced narcissi
and the whole length of the Blackwater

strengthening our embrace.

VIII. ONCE

The lovers in an Irish story never had good fortune.
They fled the king's anger. They lay on the forest floor.
They kissed at the edge of death.

Did you know our suburb was a forest?
Our roof was a home for thrushes.
Our front door was a wild shadow of spruce.

Our faces edged in mountain freshness,
we took our milk in where the wide apart
prints of the wild and never-seen
creatures were set who have long since died out.

I do not want us to be immortal or unlucky.
To listen for our own death in the distance.
Take my hand. Stand by the window:

I want to show you what is hidden in
this ordinary, ageing human love is
there still and will be until

an inland coast so densely wooded
not even the ocean fog could enter it

appears in front of us and the chilled-
to-the-bone light clears and shows us

Irish wolves: a silvery man and wife.
Yellow-eyed. Edged in dateless moonlight.
They are mated for life. They are legendary. They are safe.

IX. THANKED BE FORTUNE

Did we live a double life?

      I would have said

             we never envied

the epic glory of the star-crossed.

      I would have said

             we learned by heart

the code marriage makes of passion—

             duty dailyness routine.

But after dark when we went to bed

under the bitter fire

             of constellations—

      orderly, uninterested and cold,

             at least in our case—

in the bookshelves just above our heads,

      all through the hours of darkness,

             men and women

wept, cursed, kept and broke faith

      and killed themselves for love.

             Then it was dawn again.

Restored to ourselves,

    we woke early and lay together

listening to our child crying, as if to birdsong,

    with ice on the windowsills

        and the grass eking out

    the last crooked hour of starlight.

X. LINES FOR A THIRTIETH
WEDDING ANNIVERSARY

Somewhere up in the eaves it began:
High in the roof—in a sort of vault
between the slates and gutter—a small leak.
Through it, rain which came from the east,
in from the lights and foghorns of the coast—
water with a ghost of ocean salt in it—
spilled down on the path below.
Over and over and over
years stone began to alter,
its grain searched out, worn in:
granite rounding down, giving way,
taking into its own inertia that
information water brought: of ships,
wings, fog and phosphor in the harbor.
It happened under our lives: the rain,
the stone. We hardly noticed. Now
this is the day to think of it, to wonder:
All those years, all those years together—
the stars in a frozen arc overhead,
the quick noise of a thaw in the air,
the blue stare of the hills—through it all
this constancy: what wears, what endures.

XI. A MARRIAGE FOR THE MILLENNIUM

Do you believe
that Progress is a woman?
A spirit seeking for its opposite?
For a true marriage to ease her quick heartbeat?

I asked you this
as you sat with your glass of red wine
and your newspaper of yesterday's events.
You were drinking and reading, and did not hear me.

Then I closed the door
and left the house behind me and began
driving the whole distance of our marriage,
away from the suburb towards the city.

One by one
the glowing windows went out.
Television screens cooled down more slowly.
Ceramic turned to glass, circuits to transistors.

Old rowans were saplings.
Roads were no longer wide.
Children disappeared from their beds.
Wives, without warning, suddenly became children.

Computer games became codes again.

The codes were folded

back into the futures of their makers.

Their makers woke from sleep, weeping for milk.

When I came to the street we once lived on

with its iron edges out of another century

I stayed there only a few minutes.

Then I was in the car, driving again.

I was ready to tell you when I got home

that high above that street in a room

above the laid-out hedges and wild lilac

nothing had changed

them, nothing ever would:

The man with his creased copy of the newspaper.

Or the young woman talking to him. Talking to him.

Her heart eased by this.

II

CODE

MAKING MONEY

*At the turn of the century, the paper produced there was of
such high quality that it was exported for use as bank-note paper.*

—Dundrum and Its Environs

They made money—
                maybe not the way
you think it should be done
but they did it anyway.

At the end of summer
the rains came and braided
the river Slang as it ran down and down
the Dublin mountains and into faster water
and stiller air as if a storm was coming in.
And the mill wheel turned so the mill
could make paper and the paper money.
And the cottage doors opened and the women
came out in the ugly first hour
after dawn and began
                to cook the rags they put
hemp waste, cotton lint, linen, flax and fishnets
from boxes delivered every day on
the rag wagon on a rolling boil. And the steam rose
up from the open coils where a shoal slipped through
in an April dawn. And in the backwash they added
alkaline and caustic and soda ash and suddenly
they were making money.
              A hundred years ago

2 3

this is the way they came to the plum-brown
headlong weir and the sedge drowned in it
and their faces about to be as they looked down
once quickly on
their way to the mill, to the toil
of sifting and beating and settling and fraying
the weighed-out fibres. And they see how easily
the hemp has forgotten the Irish Sea at
neap tide and how smooth the weave is now in
their hands. And they do not and they never will

see the small boundaries all this will buy
or the poisoned kingdom with its waterways
and splintered locks or the peacocks who will walk
this paper up and down in the windless gardens
of a history no one can stop happening now.
Nor the crimson and indigo features
of the prince who will stare out from
the surfaces they have made on
the ruin of a Europe
he cannot see from the surface
of a wealth he cannot keep

                        if you can keep

your composure in the face of this final proof that
the past is not made out of time, out of memory,
out of irony but is also
a crime we cannot admit and will not atone
it will be dawn again in the rainy autumn of the year.
The air will be a skinful of water—
the distance between storms—
again. The wagon of rags will arrive.
The foreman will buy it. The boxes will be lowered to the path
the women are walking up
as they always did, as they always will now.
Facing the paradox. Learning to die of it.

So high
in their leafy silence
over Kells, over Durrow
as the Vikings
raged south—
the old monks
made the alphabet
wild:
    they dipped iron
into azure and
indigo: they gave strange
wings to their o's
and e's: their vowels
clung on with
talons and the thin
ribbed wolves
which had gone north
left their frozen winters
and were lured back
to their consonants.

CODE

An Ode to Grace Murray Hopper 1906–88
maker of a computer compiler and verifier of COBOL.

Poet to poet. I imagine you
    at the edge of language, at the start of summer
        in Wolfeboro, New Hampshire, writing code.
            You have no sense of time. No sense of minutes even.
          They cannot reach inside your world,
             your gray workstation
                with *when yet now never* and *once.*
             You have missed the other seven.
               This is the eighth day of Creation.

The peacock has been made, the rivers stocked.
The rainbow has leaned down to clothe the trout.
The earth has found its pole, the moon its tides.
Atoms, energies have done their work,
have made the world, have finished it, have rested.
And we call this Creation. And you missed it.

The line of my horizon, solid blue
    appears at last fifty years away
        from your fastidious, exact patience:
           The first sign that night will be day
              is a stir of leaves in this Dublin suburb
                and air and invertebrates and birds,
                  as the earth resorts again

to its explanations:
        Its shadows. Its reflections. Its words.

You are west of me and in the past.
Dark falls. Light is somewhere else.
The fireflies come out above the lake.
You are compiling binaries and zeroes.
The given world is what you can translate.
And you divide the lesser from the greater.

Let there be language—
    even if we use it differently:
        I never made it timeless as you have.
            I never made it numerate as you did.
                And yet I use it here to imagine
                    how at your desk in the twilight
                        legend, history and myth of course,
                            are gathering in Wolfeboro, New Hampshire,
                                as if to a memory. As if to a source.

Maker of the future, if the past
is fading from our view with the light
outside your window and the single file
of elements and animals, and all the facts

of origin and outcome, which will never find
their way to you or shelter in your syntax—

it makes no difference to us.
   We are still human. There is still light
      in my suburb and you are in my mind—
         head bowed, old enough to be my mother—
            writing code before the daylight goes.
         I am writing at a screen as blue,
            as any hill, as any lake, composing this
               to show you how the world begins again:
            One word at a time.
            One woman to another.

All night the room breathes out its grief.
Exhales through surfaces. The sideboard.
The curtains: the stale air stalled there.
The kiln-fired claws of the china bird.

This is the hour when every ornament
unloads its atoms of pretence. Stone.
Brass. Bronze. What they represent is
set aside in the dark: they become again

a spacious morning in the Comeraghs.
An iron gate; a sudden downpour; a well in
the corner of a farmyard; a pool of rain
into which an Irish world has fallen.

Out there the Americas stretch to the horizons.
They burn in the cities and darken over wheat.
They to go the edge, to the rock, to the coast,
to where the moon abrades a shabby path eastward.

O land of opportunity, you are
not the suppers with meat, nor
the curtains with lace nor the unheard of
fire in the grate on summer afternoons, you are

this room, this dish of fruit which

has never seen its own earth. Or had rain

fall on it all one night and the next. And has grown,

in consequence, a fine, crazed skin of porcelain.

young woman who climbs the stairs,
who closes a child's door,
who goes to her table
in a room at the back of a house?
The same unlighted corridor?
The same night air
over the wheelbarrows and rain-tanks?
The same inky sky and pin-bright stars?
You can see nothing of her, but her head
bent over the page, her hand moving,
moving again, and her hair.
I wrote like that once.
But this is different:
This time, when she looks up, I will be there.

If there was
a narrative to my life
in those years, then
let this
be the sound of it—
the season in, season out
sound of
the grind of
my neighbors's shears:
beautiful air of August,
music of limitation, of
the clipped
shadow and
the straightened border,
of rain on the Dublin hills,
of my children sleeping in
a simpler world:
an iron edge
the origin of order.

Tinderbox weather. Even the whins were on fire.
At dusk the ground was hard and the air dried.
A single star rose over the charred
garden hedges and whitebeams of our neighborhood.

Tinderbox faith. Those centuries in the dark—
the sinner's moving lips and patient look,
the syllables seeking a miracle—
dried to kindling: waiting in drought and silence for a spark.

August. High summer in an Irish town.
Tied sheaves and a sea haze near the ocean.
A statue of the Virgin: a passerby at her shrine
who sees her move, who sees her step down: let the blaze begin

and continue: In Ballinspittle and Kinsale
men watched as the impossible became believable.
As virgins ceased to be unavailable,
as they wept real tears under sky-blue creases and plaster veils.

I lived far away. When the sun rose over
the suburb with its slate roofs and leaf cover
news came in of a season of heat and fever
no one could remember happening before in those parts: not ever.

I leaned on the windowsill. The sky was still light.
The air had heat in it and some dew and soon the weight
of the lives we lived would become inert
house and tree shadows: odd simulacra of a summer quiet.

South of me where the roots of the lilac had died,
where fuchsia hung down over stone walls on the road
waiting for salt, waiting for rain, I understood
how deep they went—those thirsts that could not be satisfied.

And should have felt them, should have entered them. Instead
I stood at the open window: *hide this place* I said
*from angels. From the terrible regard
of those who come to find them, shelter it.*

I watched the tops of the Dublin hills burn out
all evening and the helicopters with their iron freight
and tonnage of water drop down what was not
the wild rain they had failed to imitate.

HOW WE WERE TRANSFIGURED

In those days
I never thought about
what stayed further out from
the four walls of our house.

From the hills above it.
From the sleeping children within it.

Of what lay in wait on the Irish Sea
as night moved away from it.

Of what came to us as we lay there,
held in shadows—
and shadows ourselves.

And will not come to us again.

Light the builder. Light the maker.
Fitter of roofs to gutters.
Of the tree's root to the tree's height.
And of earth to sky from the same horizon
every time:
                    assembler of openings at
the river's mouth and the mind's eye.

THE BURDENS OF A HISTORY

I

I have a reason for remembering
the unseasonable heat of that evening.

A skin of wet air on the apples.
The plane tree leaves dry as lavender.

II

We said we would not talk about the past:
About what had happened. (Which is history.)
About what could happen. (Which is fear.)

III

Then you brought a map down from the attic,
folded in such a way it fell open
at once in your hands and had the feel
of linen partly. And paper only slightly.

These were the wetlands. This was the coast.
This was our country. And already
the spidery red lines were widening
into the roads our parents drove west on

looking for signposts they had just missed.

IV

I went into a field above the city
when I was just fourteen years of age.

Before sex, before settling down,
before growing up, there was this:

Rust was everywhere, a second skin
on every inch of iron.
Distances were less ambitious.
Car parts and wheels in the ditches
seemed to say that travel was an error
whose starting point would end back here:

In this air made out of humid blues.
And the cattle which had not moved once.

V

When the storm broke they were under it.
The heat cracking. Rain hissing on the car.

They counted from the thunder on their fingers.
And waited in the freshening, lifting air
for the first strike of lightning which—
if it did not kill them—

would show them exactly where they were.

CALLED

I went to find the grave of my grandmother
who died before my time. And hers.

I searched among marsh grass and granite
and single headstones
and smashed lettering
and archangel wings and found none.

For once, I said,
I will face this landscape
and look at it as she was looked upon:

Unloved because unknown.
Unknown because unnamed:

Glass Pistol Castle disappeared.
Baltray and then Clogher Head.
To the west the estuary of the Boyne—
stripped of its battles and history—
became only willow trees and distances.

I drove back in the half-light
of late summer on
anonymous roads on my journey home

as the constellations rose overhead,

some of them twisted into women:

pinioned and winged

and single-handedly holding high the dome

and curve and horizon of today and tomorrow.

All the ships looking up to them.

All the compasses made true by them.

All the night skies named for their sorrow.

EMIGRANT LETTERS

That morning in Detroit at the airport,
after check-in, heading for the concourse,
I heard, as I was walking towards the gate—
behind me to the left—an Irish voice.

Its owner must have been away for years:
Vowels half-sounds and syllables
from somewhere else had nearly smoothed out
a way of speaking you could tell a region by,

much less an origin. I reached the gate, boarded,
closed my eyes and rose high over
towns, farms, fields—all of them at that very moment
moulding the speech of whoever lived there:

An accent overwritten by a voice. A voice
by a place. Over the waters of the coast
they were entrusted to, trying to think
of loss, I thought of them instead: emigrant letters.

Every word told and retold.
Handed over, held close, longed for and feared.
Each page six crisp inches of New England snow.
And at the end a name—half signature, half salt.

How their readers stood in cold kitchens,
heads bent, until the time came to begin again
folding over those chambers of light:
ice and owl noise and the crystal freight on

branches and fences and added them
to the stitchwort of late spring, the mosquitoes,
the unheard of heat, the wild leaves, snow again—
the overnight disappearances of wood and stone—

all of which they stored side by side
carefully in a cupboard drawer which never
would close properly: informed as it was
by those distant seasons. And warped by its own.

A MODEL SHIP MADE BY
PRISONERS LONG AGO

There it is my father said.

He put it down beside
the stack of coins
and the brass striking clock
on the mantelpiece.

A ship:
Made of parchment,
of canvas. Of foraged-for
crude glues.

Your great-grandfather
joined the Tipperary Horse.
He rose to be head of the Poorhouse.
That is, Master of the Union.

On the mantelpiece
a snipe is flying across a florin,
its base-metal wing lost to its destination
of wetlands and crabgrass.

He had fourteen children.
Eight of them survived.

He educated every one of them.
Some of them were women.

In the dark, in the stone-cold,
their fingers had threaded, moulded,
made the fo'c'sle, the hull,
then the spar and the rigging
and the promise of
a billowing main sail.

As if they could
still breathe phosphor and starlight
they had made it: a need for freedom
only visible
in what they missed:

No porpoises making a circle
of light and muscle.
No Pole Star.
No discernible line of landfall.

SUBURBAN WOMAN: ANOTHER DETAIL

I

Dusk
        and the neighborhood
is the color of shadow,
the color of stone.

Here at my desk I imagine
wintry air and the smart of peat.

And an uncurtained
front room where

another woman is living my life.
Another woman is lifting my child.

Is setting her down.
Is cutting oily rind from a lemon.
Is crushing that smell against the skin of her fingers.
She goes to my door and closes it.
Goes to my window and pulls the curtain slowly.

The kitchen,
the child she lifts again and holds

are all mine

        and all the time

the bitter, citric fragrance stays against her skin.

She stares at the road

in the featureless November twilight.

(I remember that twilight.)

Stares for a moment at

the moon which has drained it.

Then pulls the curtains shut.

And puts herself and my child beyond it.

II

I can see nothing now.

I write at my desk alone.

I choose words taken from the earth,

from the root, from the faraway

oils and essence of elegy:

Bitter. And close to the bone.

HOW WE MADE A NEW ART ON OLD GROUND

A famous battle happened in this valley.
            You never understood the nature poem.
Till now. Till this moment—if these statements
            seem separate, unrelated, follow this

silence to its edge and you will hear
            the history of air: the crispness of a fern
or the upward cut and turn around of
            a fieldfare or thrush written on it.

The other history is silent. The estuary
            is over there. The issue was decided here:
Two kings prepared to give no quarter.
            Then one king and one dead tradition.

Now the humid dusk, the old wounds
            wait for language, for a different truth.
When you see the silk of the willow
            and the wider edge of the river turn

and grow dark and then darker, then
            you will know that the nature poem
is not the action nor its end: it is
            this rust on the gate beside the trees, on

the cattle grid underneath our feet,
                on the steering wheel shaft: it is
an aftermath, an overlay and even in
                its own modest way, an art of peace:

I try the word *distance* and it fills with
                sycamores, a summer's worth of pollen
And as I write *valley* straw, metal
                blood, oaths, armor are unwritten.

Silence spreads slowly from these words
                to those ilex trees half in, half out
of shadows falling on the shallow ford
                of the south bank beside Yellow island

as twilight shows how this sweet corrosion
                begins to be complete: what we see
is what the poem says:
                evening coming—cattle, cattle-shadows—

and whin bushes and a change of weather
                about to change them all: what we see is how
the place and the torment of the place are
                for this moment free of one another.

THE OLD CITY

Small things
make the past.
Make the present seem out of place.

A woman cracking and twisting.
Black atoms falling down
on green leaves.

If I am ever to go back
to what I loved first
here are words to be wished on—

(almost, you can see, an incantation).

Summon blue air
out of a corridor between
a mountain range and a sea
(this at least has never changed).

Empty out the streets.
Fit the cars easily
into their parking places.
Slow the buses down by thirty years.

Observe a brave, fiery shower
above a plate
of bacon and potatoes

(we are nearly there).

Now say *dinner* for *lunch*.
And *teatime* instead of *supper*.

And see how it comes again—

My little earth.

My city of white pepper.

IRISH POETRY

for Michael Hartnett

We always knew there was no Orpheus in Ireland.
No music stored at the doors of hell.
No god to make it.
No wild beasts to weep and lie down to it.

But I remember an evening when the sky
was underworld-dark at four,
when ice had seized every part of the city
and we sat talking—
the air making a wreath for our cups of tea.

And you began to speak of our own gods.
Our heartbroken pantheon.

No Attic light for them and no Herodotus.
But thin rain and dogfish and the stopgap
of the sharp cliffs
they spent their winters on.

And the pitch-black Atlantic night:
how the sound
of a bird's wing in a lost language sounded.

You made the noise for me.

Made it again.

Until I could see the flight of it: suddenly

the silvery lithe rivers of the southwest
lay down in silence
and the savage acres no one could predict
were all at ease, soothed and quiet and
listening to you, as I was. As if to music, as if to peace.